For Reference

Not to be taken from this room

Riches of the Earth

Iron

Irene Franck and David Brownstone

GROLIER
An imprint of Scholastic Library Publishing
Danbury, Connecticut

Credits and Acknowledgments

abbreviations: t (top), b (bottom), l (left), r (right), c (center)
Image credits: Art Resource: 18 (Scala), 19 (detail) and 20l (Erich Lessing), 22 (Victoria and Albert Museum); Bethlehem Steel Corporation: 1b, 4, 9b, 10t, 10b, 21, 23, 27, 28t, 28c, 28b, 29; Bridgeman Art Library: 6 (Yale Center for British Art); Fort McHenry: 24; Getty Images/Foodpix: 7 (Push); Getty Images/PhotoDisc: 11 (Erin Hogan), 12 (David Chasey), 16 (Adalberto Rios Szalay/Sexto Sol); Library of Congress: 3, 25; National Aeronautics and Space Administration (NASA): 1t and running heads; Photo Researchers, Inc.: 9t (Oliver Meckes/Eye of Science), 13 (Dr. Gopal Murti/Science Photo Library), 15 (Holt Studios International/Nigel Cattlin); U.S. Department of Agriculture: 14; Woodfin Camp & Associates: 5 (George Olson), 8 (Eastcott/Momatiuk), 20r (detail) (Jonathan Blair). Original image drawn for this book by K & P Publishing Services: 17.

Our thanks to Joe Hollander, Phil Friedman, and Laurie McCurley at Scholastic Library Publishing; to photo researchers Susan Hormuth, Robin Sand, and Robert Melcak; to copy editor Michael Burke; and to the librarians throughout the northeastern library network, in particular to the staff of the Chappaqua Library—director Mark Hasskarl; the expert reference staff, including Martha Alcott, Michele J. Capozzella, Maryanne Eaton, Catherine Paulsen, Jane Peyraud, Paula Peyraud, and Carolyn Reznick; and the circulation staff, headed by Barbara Le Sauvage—for fulfilling our wide-ranging research needs.

Published 2003 by Grolier
Division of Scholastic Library Publishing
Old Sherman Turnpike
Danbury, Connecticut 06816

For information address the publisher:
Scholastic Library Publishing, Grolier Division
Old Sherman Turnpike, Danbury, Connecticut 06816

© 2003 Irene M. Franck and David M. Brownstone

All rights reserved. Except for use in a review, no part of this book may be reproduced, stored in a retrieval system, or transmitted in any form, or by any means, electronic or mechanical, including photocopying, recording, or otherwise, without prior permission of Scholastic Library Publishing.

Library of Congress Cataloging-in-Publication Data

Franck, Irene M.
    Iron / Irene Franck and David Brownstone.
      p. cm. -- (Riches of the earth ; v. 5)
    Summary: Provides information about iron and its importance in everyday life.
    Includes bibliographical references and index.
    ISBN 0-7172-5730-4 (set : alk. paper) -- ISBN 0-7172-5717-7 (vol. 5 : alk paper)
      1. Iron--Juvenile literature [1. Iron.] I. Brownstone, David M. II. Title.

TN705.F73 2003
669'.141--dc21

2003044081

Printed in the United States of America

Designed by K & P Publishing Services

Contents

Iron All Around 4

What Is Iron? 6

Iron Reacts 8

   Iron or Fe 9

Iron and Magnetism 11

Iron for Life 13

Where Is Iron Found? 16

The Early Iron Age 18

   Early Steel 22

The Modern Age of Iron 23

Words to Know 30

On the Internet 31

In Print 31

Index 32

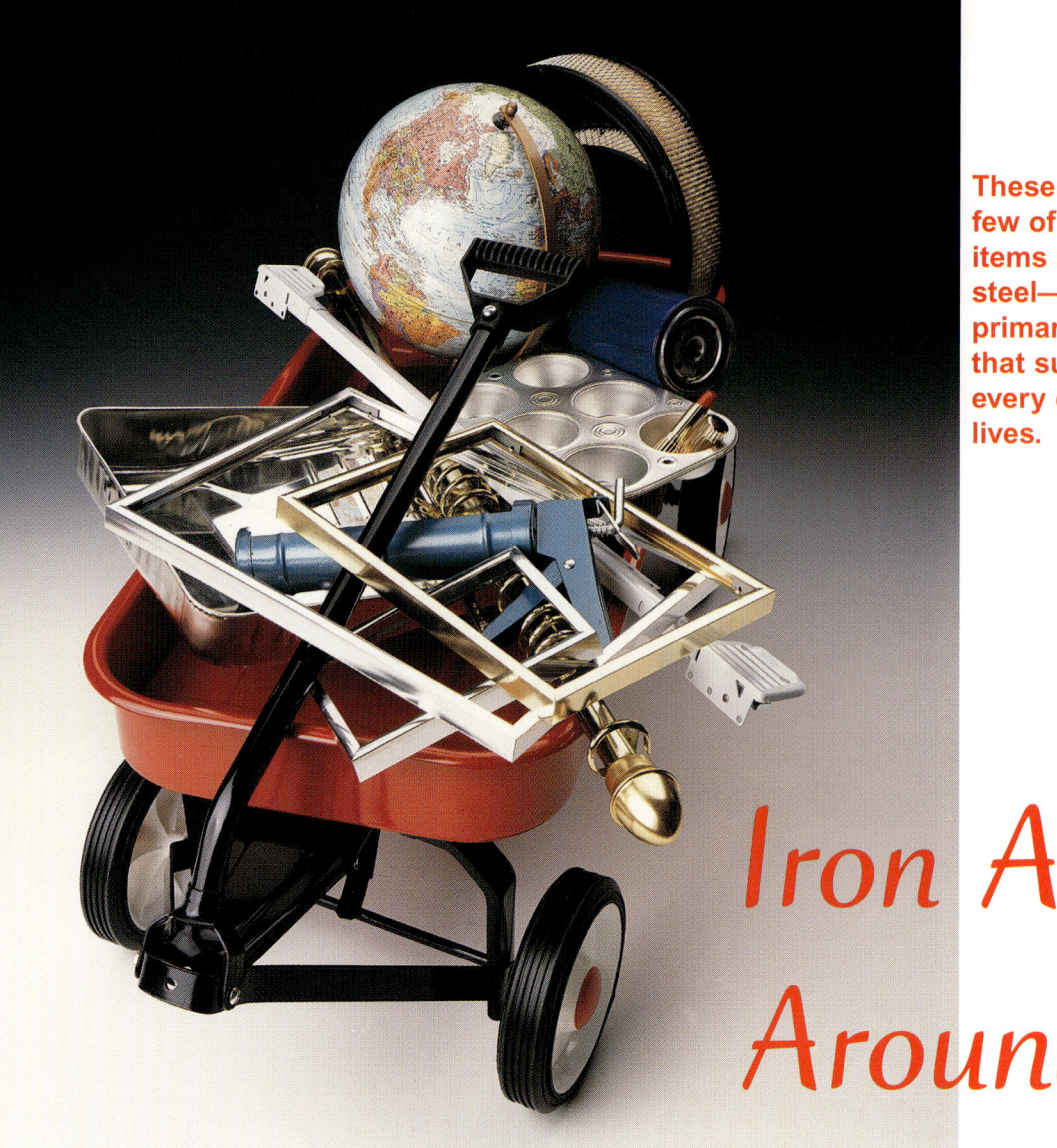

These are just a few of the many items made of steel—which is primarily iron—that surround us every day of our lives.

Iron All Around

Iron is everywhere, inside us and all around us. Plants and animals of every size and shape—even tiny bacteria—need iron to grow and survive. Iron is essential to life on Earth (see p. 13).

We humans are partly made of iron. So is the Earth at its very core. Iron is also found in many different forms in the crust of the Earth, the outer layer where we live.

Iron is also all around us in everyday life because it is enormously useful. From the largest skyscrapers to your local school or shopping center, the frames of most large buildings today are made of steel, which is primarily iron.

But iron is not only used for large structures. Whenever you play an audiotape or videocassette, tiny bits of iron trigger the signals you hear and see. This is possible because iron is easily magnetized

Iron All Around

Early trains were sometimes called *iron horses*, since the steam-driven engines were largely made of black iron.

(see p. 11), so pieces can readily be put in either "on" or "off" positions for storing all kinds of data. Iron is also the basis for many other everyday items, from sewing needles to stainless steel tableware to "tin" cans (actually tin-covered steel). Iron is also part of many colors used in paints.

Ages of Iron

Iron has been so important that more than one historical period has been named after it. The first came in early times, when humans first learned how to smelt (melt and purify) iron. That led to what archaeologists call the Iron Age. The new, cheaper, stronger tools and weapons made with iron helped change human civilization (see p. 18).

The second Age of Iron came in modern times, starting in the 19th century, when people learned how to make higher-quality iron and steel (see p. 23). Small amounts of carbon and other materials added to iron to form steel make it even stronger. Indeed, this modern Iron Age might better be named an Age of Steel.

5

Blacksmiths, who work with iron, have been regarded with awe and fascination for centuries. People have often gathered to watch them work, as in this late-1700s painting, *The Blacksmith's Shop* by Joseph Wright of Derby. Some early people even had a god who was a metalsmith, known as Hephaestus by the Greeks and Vulcan by the Romans.

What Is Iron?

Iron is one of the most common materials on Earth. It makes up at least 5 percent of the Earth's crust.

Everything on the Earth—living and nonliving—is made up of some basic substances called *elements*. (Scientists have discovered 112 elements so far, though more are being discovered.) Of these elements iron is the fourth most common found in the crust, after oxygen, silicon, and aluminum.

However, iron makes up about 35 percent of the Earth as a whole. That is because the core of the Earth—at its center, beginning about 1,800 miles (2,900 kilometers) below the surface—is about 90 percent iron.

Iron as a Metal

Iron is one of a group of elements called *metals*. Many metals are very useful because heat and electricity readily flow through them (scientists call them *good conductors*). They can also be shaped into many useful things. Metals are solid at room temperature and can often be hammered into many

What Is Iron?

kinds of shapes. They can also be melted at high temperatures and then poured into molds of desired shapes. All of those things are true of iron. Indeed, it is the hardest of all the easy-to-work metals.

Most metals also readily join with other elements to form new mixed materials called *compounds*. Iron is so ready to form compounds that it is rarely found in its pure silvery-white form. Instead, it is found in hundreds of different kinds of compounds, commonly black or reddish-brown.

When two metals join together, the compound is called an *alloy*. Iron alloys, especially steel, play a central role in our modern world (see p. 23). Iron also has a special and important property called *magnetism* (see p. 11).

Iron is by far the most widely used metal, making up about 90 percent of all the metal products in the 21st century. That is because iron is the easiest metal to find, mine, and process (see p. 16), and the resulting objects are often strong and hard.

In living things iron is far from common. An adult human body contains only three to five grams of iron, about as much as is in a small nail. However, this iron has life-and-death importance (see p. 13).

Iron spreads heat so fully and evenly that it has long been favored in cooking. Many cooks still prefer cast-iron frying pans like this one, though other metals are now often used in pots and pans.

When iron is not kept clean and dry, it rusts quickly, especially in the sea air. This anchor is covered with reddish-brown rust, which has sent orange streaks down the side of an abandoned boat.

Iron Reacts

Iron is a very active element. Chemists call it *reactive*. That means that iron readily combines with other substances to form new ones.

Reactivity can be both a strength and a weakness. Iron is used for many purposes because it easily forms new compounds (see p. 7). Many of these include the element oxygen and are called *oxides*.

However, iron reacts so readily that it also forms unwanted compounds.

The classic example is *rust*. Rust is actually one of a series of compounds that include different amounts of iron and oxygen. These are called *ferric oxides* (see box on p. 9).

One form of ferric oxide is enormously useful. It is used in record-

 Iron Reacts

To the naked eye this nail would look shiny, with only a trace of rust. But if you look at it here, magnified 550 times, you can see that the surface is covered with iron-and-oxygen compounds we call *rust*.

ing audio- or videocassettes (see p. 4) as well as in forming colors for paints and polishes for metal.

However, in the presence of water and air, objects made of iron can easily form rust—that is, the iron at the surface combines with oxygen. The object's surface then turns crumbly and a dark reddish-brown, making it less strong and hard.

People have tried different ways to prevent rust. One approach is to cover the surface. Painting an iron fence, for example, keeps rust from forming—until the paint peels away and needs to be replaced. For commercial uses iron may be coated with another substance. Iron coated with the element zinc is called *galvanized iron*. Another approach is to add substances to iron, forming new rust-resistant compounds or

Molten iron is here being poured into a furnace to be made into steel.

Iron or Fe

The early Romans—whose language was Latin—knew iron as *ferrum*. During the Middle Ages Europeans began to speak different languages in their everyday lives. However, people in universities continued for centuries to use Latin in their writing and scientific work. Many of the new iron compounds that scientists discovered were named with forms of the word *ferrum*. That is why the modern chemical abbreviation for iron is *Fe* and the names of many iron compounds include the words *ferrous*, *ferric*, or *ferro-*.

9

In the 1700s iron began to be used for bridges and other structures, at first small ones like the ones at the right. However, as steelmaking methods improved and steel became stronger, bridges and other buildings became higher and larger such as Rhode Island's Newport Bridge shown above. However, the bridges must be kept carefully painted, so they do not rust and become weakened.

alloys, such as stainless steel (see p. 27).

Why is iron so active and reactive? The answer lies in its structure.

Everything on the Earth is made up of tiny basic units called *atoms*. In an element, such as iron, all the atoms are alike. Atoms are made up of even smaller particles. The particles mainly responsible for chemical reactions are called *electrons*. When substances "react" with each other, they give up or receive electrons.

Because of its pattern of electrons, iron is unusually ready to exchange electrons with other substances.

Electricity—the power that drives our modern world—is actually made up of a flow of electrons. Electrons flow easily through iron, so it is called a good *conductor*. That's why iron compounds are so often found in wires and other electrical parts. Electrons are also important in magnetism (see p. 11).

With a small magnet you can pick up paperclips and other light items. But with a huge magnet a machine can pick up a whole car!

Iron and Magnetism

From at least 500 B.C. humans recognized that a type of rock they called *lodestone* attracted (pulled toward itself) certain other rocks. Today we know this as the iron-bearing rock *magnetite* (see p. 16), and the power of attraction is called *magnetism*.

Magnetism involves a flow of electrons (see p. 10). Only a few substances show strong magnetic power, and iron is by far the strongest.

Anything magnetic has two different poles, generally labeled north and south. When like poles (north-north or south-south) are brought together, they repel (push away) each other. However, opposite poles (north-south) attract each other.

Indeed, because it contains so much iron, the Earth itself is a magnet, with north and south poles. Any object that is magnetized tends to line up in the same north-south direction, so that its south pole points to the Earth's north pole.

This is the basis of the direction-finding device called the *compass*. The earliest compass, dating from at

Iron

least the 1100s, was probably a piece of lodestone placed on wood floating on water. The lodestone would line up in a north-south direction, pointing the way north. Later compasses used iron or steel needles to find north.

Today iron's magnetism has many uses. Huge magnets move heavy pieces of scrap metal, such as old cars. Tiny iron magnets are used in switches, relays, and other types of control and storage devices, including computers and tape players. These tiny bits of iron can be magnetized in "on" and "off" positions, storing all kinds of information.

Magnetism is actually part of a more general force called *electromagnetism*. Magnetism is used to produce flows of electricity, as in generators and motors. It also creates the patterns of electrically charged particles that form pictures on a television screen.

In medicine a technique called *magnetic resonance imaging* (MRI) analyzes magnetic shifts in the cells in the body. These can help identify problems such as tumors.

In all of these and many other uses, iron plays a key role.

Using the compass, navigators have sailed the far seas and hikers have been able to find their way. That's because the compass's magnetic needle always points the way north.

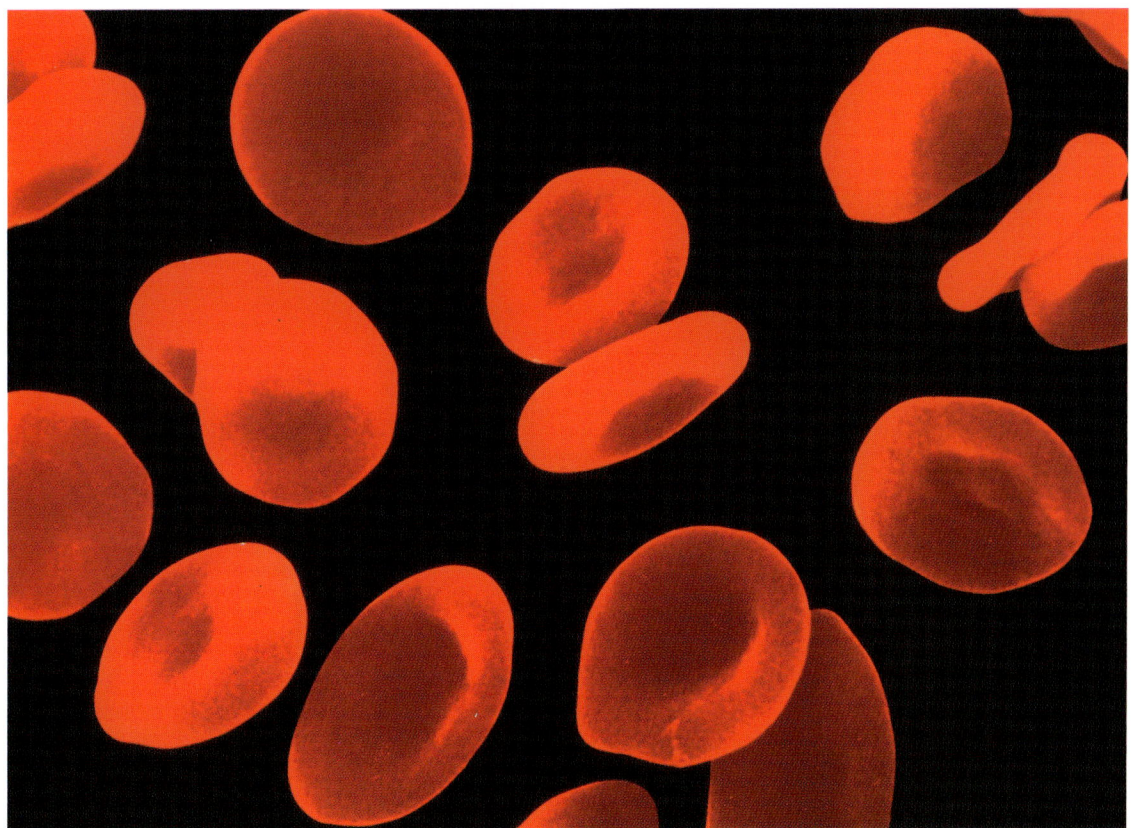

Iron and oxygen give blood its well-known bright red color. Seventy percent of the body's iron is used in red blood cells like these, magnified over 2,200 times. Traveling through your body delivering oxygen, a red blood cell might travel nine or ten miles a day!

Iron for Life

Iron is necessary for human life. Every moment that we are alive, we must breathe in a gas called *oxygen*. Iron is the "ferry" that carries oxygen throughout our bodies. Iron does this because it readily joins with oxygen (see p. 8).

It works like this: Red blood cells contain *hemoglobin*, a material that includes iron. Blood carries these red blood cells to the lungs. There iron "picks up" oxygen. The blood then flows throughout the body, "dropping off" oxygen wherever it is needed, before returning to the lungs for more oxygen. Much the same process takes place in many other animals.

Iron is also necessary for many other functions in the bodies of

Dark green vegetables like this bunch of kale can give you some of the iron that your body needs every day.

humans and other living beings. These include providing energy for the body and rebuilding cells.

Iron is so important that some of it is held in reserve. In humans almost 30 percent of the iron is stored in body tissues, especially in the liver and heart.

Each red blood cell lasts for only about three months, so the body is constantly making new ones. It uses iron from old red blood cells but also some new iron.

To meet the body's daily need for iron, a person must take in 10 to 20 milligrams each day. Otherwise the body will need to tap its iron reserves.

However, if the reserves are tapped too often, the body will run low on iron. That can happen, for example, when someone is starving, loses a lot of blood, is pregnant, or is growing rapidly. People who are low on iron have *iron-deficiency anemia*. The most obvious sign of this condition is that someone feels "run down."

The best way to restore the body's iron reserves is to eat iron-rich foods, such as red meat, green leafy vegetables, dried fruits, beans, and whole-grain breads and cereals. Some foods are also *enriched* with iron, meaning that iron has been added to them.

If plants do not get enough iron, their leaves—instead of being bright or dark green—will turn yellowish-green. That is what has happened to some of the leaves on this rhododendron bush.

Some people also take iron pills. They must be cautious, however, for too much iron can be dangerous. It can build up in the body's organs, causing a condition called *iron overload*. People with bleeding disorders, who receive blood transfusions, can also build up too much iron. Also some people's bodies do not handle iron properly, producing an inherited form of iron overload.

In severe cases of iron overload, iron is even deposited in skin tissues, giving the skin a bronze color, as in a deep tan. Some people's bodies contain so much iron that they set off metal detectors in airports! Iron overload can damage the heart, liver, and other organs and can even lead to death.

Plants are very different from animals, but they also need iron. The amounts are small. However, if a plant does not have enough iron, it will not grow properly. Such plants often turn yellowish-green, instead of the normal bright green. This condition is called *chlorosis*, from the Greek word meaning "pale green." Farmers sometimes supply iron to their crops to help them grow better.

Even tiny one-celled organisms need iron. Indeed, bacteria and other smaller organisms play an important role in bringing iron to plants.

Because iron is so widely available, it is most often mined at or near the surface, as here in Venezuela.

Where Is Iron Found?

Iron is found in many parts of the world. It is almost always combined with other elements in materials called *ores*. Some elements can make iron stronger, but others make it weaker and are hard to separate out. The trick is to find convenient deposits of easy-to-separate high-iron ores.

The most useful iron ore is *hematite*. Hematite is often reddish-black or brick-red, the color most often associated with iron mines and processing plants. *Magnetite* is another very useful ore. Strongly magnetic (see p. 11), this black rock contains more iron than hematite but is not found as widely.

Some *meteorites* (rocks from space) are as much as 90 percent iron, some of it nearly pure. This was the source of some of the earliest iron tools and weapons (see p. 18). Early people called it the "metal from the heavens."

Sources of Iron Ores

The Earth's iron-rich core is so hot that it is in molten (melted) form. Over many millions of years some molten material reached the surface

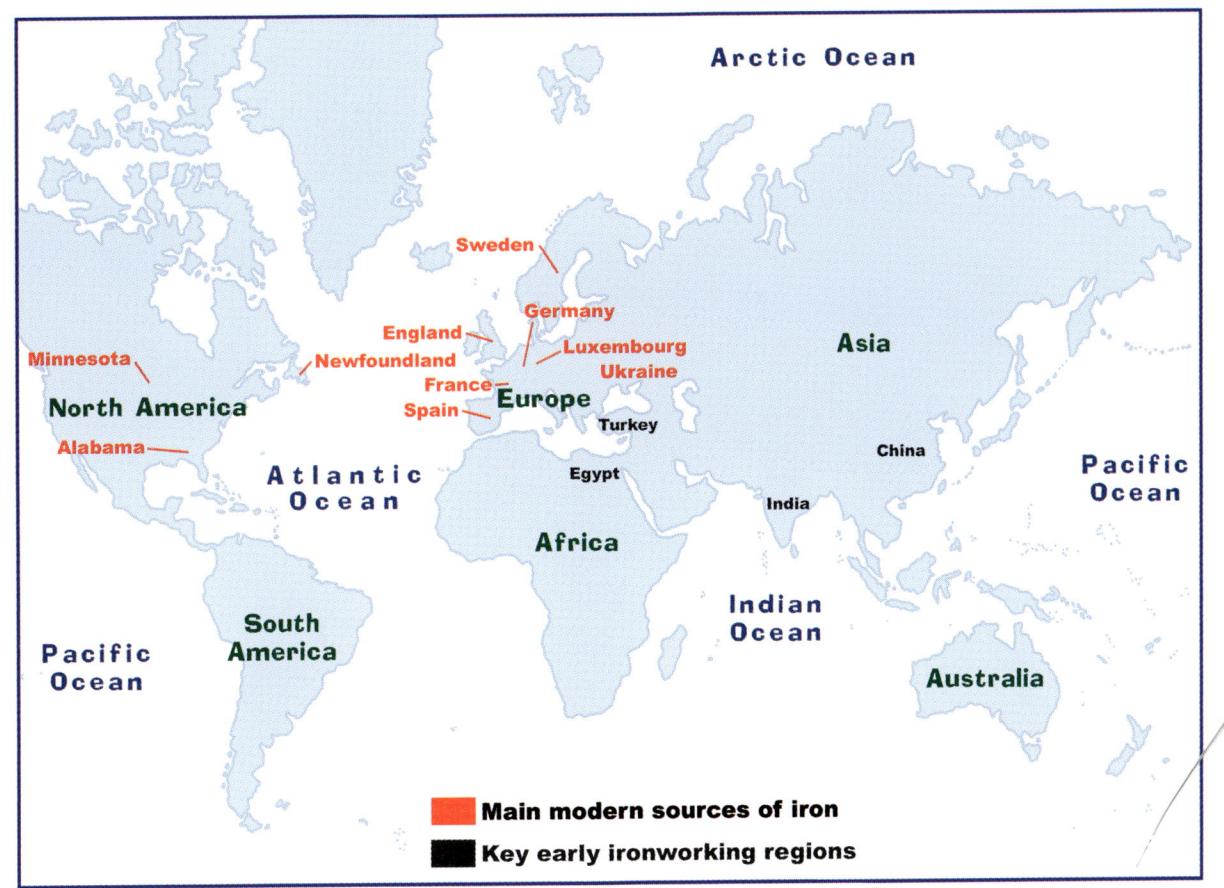

and cooled to form rocks in the Earth's crust. Hematite and magnetite were originally formed in this way.

Over time, however, many such rocks were worn down and broken apart by water, air, rain, and other natural forces in the process called *erosion*. The iron particles freed from such eroded rocks massed together below ancient swamps, lakes, and seas. There they formed new rock deposits.

That process continues today. A brown, earthy iron ore called *limonite* is often found underneath swamps, marshes, or seashores.

Iron-bearing deposits are found all around the world. Even today, most iron is mined at or near the surface. As a result, most peoples in early times had enough iron for their local purposes.

Modern industry requires larger deposits. The main modern sources for iron have included England's Midlands region, Spain's Bilbao deposits, Minnesota's Mesabi Range, Ukraine's Krivoi Rog region, Germany's Ruhr region, Alabama's Clinton mines, France's Lorraine region, Newfoundland's Wabana mines, Sweden's Kiruna region, and Luxembourg (see map above).

The reds and browns in early cave paintings often were made from iron compounds. This prehistoric image of a bison (buffalo) comes from Spain's Santimamine Caves.

The Early Iron Age

Humans were using iron by 35,000 B.C. as part of colored paints in cave paintings. (Some iron-based colors—especially reds, yellows, and browns—had been used long, long before then.) However, it would be many centuries before humans recognized iron as a separate substance.

At some time between 5000 and 4500 B.C., people in the Near East learned how to melt ores (see p. 16) to separate out useful metals, a process called *smelting*. The first smelted metal was copper, which was then used to make tools and weapons (earlier made from stone and sometimes wood and bone).

By about 3100 B.C. people in the Middle East had learned how to mix together two metals—tin and copper—to form the alloy *bronze*. Harder

The Early Iron Age

than copper and easier to melt and shape, bronze was soon preferred for tools and weapons.

Beginnings of Ironworking

Small iron objects, including jewelry, were made by 2200 B.C. from iron found in meteorites (see p. 16). While smelting other ores, some metalworkers may have accidentally smelted iron as early as 2000 B.C. This could happen when a fire was built on top of iron-bearing rocks, which then partly melted. With their small fires, however, early humans could make only low-quality iron, inferior to bronze. Their iron objects were for decorative or ceremonial use.

Ironworking techniques gradually improved. By 1500 B.C. metalworkers in what is now Turkey were making iron weapons. (Some archaeologists call this the beginning of an "Iron Age.") These early ironworkers tried to keep their techniques secret. Even so, by around 1200 B.C. iron was being worked throughout the Middle East.

Some early smelters built their fires in a hole dug in the ground, called a *bowl furnace*. Others used a *shaft furnace*, a stone-built fireplace topped by a vertical air passage (shaft).

In these furnaces iron ore was mixed and burned with charcoal (a carbon-rich material, often wood, already partly burned to make it a hotter-burning fuel.) Air—containing oxygen needed for burning the charcoal—was often blown in through pipes (*tuyeres*). Later ironworkers added *bellows* (devices for forcing more air into a fire) made of animal skins to the pipes.

However, the fires were not hot enough to reach iron's melting point: 1,536 degrees Celsius (about 2,800 Fahrenheit). Instead these furnaces produced a spongy lump of partly melted iron called a *bloom*, which was removed from the furnace for later use. The bloom also contained unwanted matter (*slag*), including pieces of charcoal.

People using weapons tipped with iron had a significant advantage over people with weapons of bronze, stone, or bone. These iron arrowheads were used by people in what is now Germany more than 2,500 years ago.

Iron

More than 2,500 years ago, a blacksmith made and used these tools in what is now the Czech Republic. The object at the upper left is an ingot (bar) of iron, which could later be reheated and hammered into a tool like those shown here.

In early Europe a special class of blacksmith emerged to make the elaborate coats of armor worn from Roman times on, including helmets like this one from the Mediterranean island of Cyprus. Each was made by hand, often to fit a particular person.

To remove the bloom, early ironworkers often had to break open a section of the furnace. This meant that they had to rebuild the furnace before smelting more ore.

Wrought Iron

Ironworkers later reheated the bloom to red-hot temperatures and hammered it into the desired shapes. This process also removed some of the slag. The result was *wrought iron*. (Wrought is an old-fashioned word for *worked*.) Strong and easily hammered into all sorts of useful objects, wrought iron would be the main form of iron used into the 19th century. It is generally black, so ironworkers would be called *blacksmiths*.

Iron is stronger than bronze, so peoples armed with iron weapons had a major advantage over those who did not. During this early Iron

The Early Iron Age

Age iron-armed peoples swept throughout much of Europe and Asia. Their movements would change history.

These peoples helped spread knowledge of how to smelt and work with iron. However, some peoples, most notably in the Americas, would make little or no use of iron until modern times.

Another advantage of iron was that it was so readily available. This meant that far more people could have iron tools or weapons—though sometimes only the top or edge would be of iron. Iron axes and plows made land easier to clear and farm, and more people settled in permanent homes.

Cast Iron

Sometimes early ironworkers accidentally produced *cast iron*, a form of iron that contains more carbon (roughly 2 to 4.5 percent). This might have happened when extra charcoal was mixed into the smelting fire. The additional carbon low-

When heated to its melting point, iron turns red and white hot. Other unwanted material called *slag* forms dark crusty masses around the edges, as here where molten iron is being stirred in a modern furnace.

Iron

ers iron's melting point, so iron can be fully melted in a small fire. The molten iron can then be *cast* (poured into molds of the desired shapes).

Casting iron was far easier than the hammering needed for wrought iron. However, cast iron is more brittle (likely to crack or break). Over the centuries some ironworkers would learn to strengthen cast iron by slowly reheating it (*tempering*) and then plunging it into cold water or other liquid (*quenching*).

However, only the Chinese routinely made and used cast iron until modern times. Starting in about 400 B.C., the Chinese also developed increasingly effective bellows. The Chinese would use cast iron in construction for centuries before such uses appeared in the West (see p. 25).

Early Steel

Steel is a form of iron that has very small amounts of carbon (less than 2 percent). Like cast iron, early steel was hard but brittle. However, it could be made stronger and more flexible by tempering and quenching (see above).

Some steels are made stronger by the addition of other materials. These can be included by accident, depending on the type of iron ore being smelted. As a result, steels made in some regions were far stronger than those made elsewhere.

Some steel was made in Egypt by 900 B.C. and in China by 200 B.C. However, the first major production came some centuries later, when ironworkers in India produced *wootz steel*. This involved hammering the bloom to remove slag and then baking it in a sealed clay container with wood chips, which absorbed some carbon.

Wootz steel was used to make the famous Damascus swords. These also underwent a tempering process for strength. However, no one knows precisely how they were made. Steel was only made on a small scale until the mid-1900s (see p. 23).

This dagger of Damascus steel dates from about 1600.

This is the classic profile of a blast furnace: Iron ore, coke, and limestone from nearby storage fields are carried in carts up a trackway (the slanted pieces in this image) to the top of the furnace and dumped in. As they travel down through the furnace, the heat gradually melts the iron, which pours out of a taphole at the bottom. Except when being cleaned or repaired, blast furnaces generally run day and night. This one is from Bethlehem Steel's Sparrow's Point plant near Baltimore, Maryland.

The Modern Age of Iron

Over the centuries iron-smelting furnaces grew larger. By the 1400s European ironworkers had begun to use waterpower to drive bellows forcing air into furnaces. This created a hotter smelting fire. Even so, most furnaces still produced only small blooms for wrought iron.

Blast Furnaces

During the 1400s (possibly earlier) the *blast furnace* was developed in Europe. Its taller shaft could take more charcoal, producing fires hot enough to make cast iron (see p. 21).

In a blast furnace, molten iron sinks to the bottom and is removed through a taphole. In early blast furnaces it poured out into a wide channel and then into smaller channels sticking out from the side. There iron cooled into bars called *pigs* (because the arrangement resembled an adult female pig nursing her piglets). Bars of pig iron could be stored until needed, then

23

Iron

remelted and cast into molds of the desired shape.

The blast furnace could produce larger amounts of iron than bloomery furnaces. Cast iron was especially desired for making guns and, from the mid-1500s, cannons.

Changing Times

Iron was still used on a small scale. Blacksmiths worked in every village, making iron products one by one. They needed iron that they could hammer into desired shapes, from hinges and horseshoes to pots and pans. As a result, large amounts of cast iron were converted into lumps for wrought iron by a process called *fining*.

Blast furnaces, bloomeries, fineries, and blacksmith shops—all used charcoal as their main fuel. However, the demand for charcoal soon outstripped the supply.

Cast-iron weapons changed the face of modern warfare. These are cannons at Fort McHenry, where Francis Scott Key wrote "The Star-Spangled Banner" during the War of 1812.

The Modern Age of Iron

These are workers at the Paterson Iron Company in Paterson, New Jersey, in the 1860s. The company specialized in making iron pieces for steamboats and railroads.

Starting in 1709, Englishman Abraham Darby first used *coke* (coal partly burned to make it a better fuel) in smelting iron. This allowed larger blast furnaces. Furnaces grew larger yet when steam engines were used to blow more air into the fire.

The Industrial Revolution

Iron laid the basis for the major social transformation called the *Industrial Revolution*. Traditionally most products were made as needed. That began to change in the 1700s when English inventors developed spinning machines. Instead of being spun and woven at home, textiles were made in large buildings called *factories*. Many of the early machines in this revolution were made of iron.

Throughout human history, most products had been made by individual craft workers. However, in the late 1790s American Eli Whitney realized that parts could be made ahead of time in standard shapes and sizes. Then unspecialized workers could quickly assemble those parts into a finished product.

Iron was ideally suited to Whitney's concept, because it could easily be cast into molds of specific shapes. Iron could also readily be formed into machines to make identical parts from other substances, such as a lathe used to carve wood into a desired shape. The results were truly revolutionary.

Cast iron also began being used for construction in the West (as it had been earlier in China; see p. 22). The first major cast-iron structure was Ironbridge, built across England's Severn River in 1779.

Cast iron was used in frames for buildings, with some rising to five stories or more for the first time.

25

Iron

Cast iron was also used in making early railroad engines—called *iron horses*—and the tracks they ran on.

Soon, however, cast iron and wrought iron would both be largely replaced by steel in construction and most other uses. Cast iron would have only special uses, as in cooking ware. Wrought iron would become primarily a decorative metal, as in fences and gates.

The Age of Steel

The modern age of steel began in 1856, when American Henry Bessemer developed a large-scale process for converting pig iron to steel. Steel is much stronger and more flexible than cast iron or wrought iron, so it would largely replace both.

Steel starts with pig iron. Small amounts of carbon (up to 2 percent) and various other substances are added to make it even stronger. Various kinds of steel—each with its own "recipe"—have been developed for different purposes. Sometimes steels are known by the main added element, such as *chromium steel*, but sometimes by their main use.

Mild steel has small amounts of manganese and silicon added. This is the main kind of steel used in construction, as in bridges, ships, water pipes, electricity pylons, and building frames, and in making large products such as auto bodies and refrigerators. Mild steel is also used to make many containers, from the huge ones carried on cargo ships to "tin cans," which are made of steel coated with tin.

Mild steel must be coated in some way to protect against rust (see p. 8). Nickel and molybdenum are sometimes added to make it even harder and less likely to rust, but they also make it more expensive.

Alloy steel includes larger amounts (3 to 5 percent) of added elements, such as nickel, chromium, vanadium, niobium, and molybdenum. Heat-treated for strength, it is used to make crankshafts, gears, motors, pumps, and the like.

Tool steel has even larger amounts (up to 10 percent) of added elements, such as tungsten, vanadium, and molybdenum. It is used to make cutting tools, including those on machines that cut and shape metals.

Stainless steel includes much larger amounts of chromium (about 18 percent) and nickel (8 to 10 percent). This is widely used in kitchens and tableware, for medical and dental instruments, and on decorative work exposed to the air, such as on the outside of skyscrapers or automobiles.

Modern Steel Plants

Modern steel plants are enormous operations. Brought in from

The Modern Age of Iron

mines, iron ore is crushed to the right size, carried to the top of the blast furnace, and poured in, along with coke (often produced at the same plant) and limestone to help the process along. Heat from the fire burns the coke and melts the iron as the mixture travels down through the furnace. At the end, pig iron pours out the bottom.

Pig iron, with other elements added, is then converted into steel. In the mid-20th century about 90 percent of all steel was made in gas-heated open-hearth furnaces. Like cooks, steelworkers test samples of the steel, to see if it is properly done. This is the classic image of steel-working.

However, by the late 20th cen-

Molten iron from a blast furnace is here being poured from a huge container into a basic oxygen furnace (BOF), where it will be converted into steel.

27

Much steel intended for later use is flattened into long sheets and then rolled up into large coils while still hot, as in this Bethlehem Steel plant (as pictured at left). Later they will cool into silver-colored coils (as pictured below) that can be readily shipped, stored, and then used for many different kinds of purposes.

Sheets of steel are sometimes coated with other materials to prevent them from rusting. Much of the food that we eat and drink every day comes in tin cans like these, which are actually made of steel coated with tin.

tury most steel was being made in newer types of furnaces. The basic oxygen furnace (BOF) uses nearly pure oxygen and is 10 times faster than the open-hearth. The electric-arc furnace, heated by electricity, is even more efficient in energy and cost. It is often used for making special steel.

In addition to pig iron, scrap steel is today often used in making new steel. Both the basic oxygen

28

The Modern Age of Iron

and electric-arc furnaces can take far more scrap steel than the open-hearth furnace can.

From the furnace some molten steel is poured directly into special-purpose molds, to form such things as the teeth on bulldozers or the frames of large engines. Some is slightly cooled and then pressed into the desired shape, a process called *forging*, after the blacksmith's forge (hearth). Some is drawn through holes to form wire.

However, most steel is sent for shaping to a *rolling mill*. It can be poured into huge molds to form *ingots*, which are cooled and then later reheated at the rolling mill. Or the molten steel may be poured into a special open-ended cooling mold. This process, called *continuous casting*, feeds the steel directly to the rolling mill, so no reheating is needed.

At the rolling mill, rollers can be set to produce thick slabs of steel cut to specific lengths, or long, flat sheets that are coiled into a roll. These slabs or sheets are quenched in water and sent to factories for later use. Sometimes the rollers have grooves and ridges to form products of specific shapes, such as the steel girders used in building skyscrapers (as shown on p. 1).

Steel girders like these form the basic "skeleton" of modern skyscrapers. These construction workers are putting together girders for a new high-rise building.

Words to Know

alloy A COMPOUND that includes two or more METALS, such as STEEL.

atom A basic "building block" of nature. In an ELEMENT, such as iron, all the atoms are alike.

blacksmith Traditional name for an ironworker.

carbon One of the main ELEMENTS in the universe. Different forms of iron contain varying amounts of carbon (see CAST IRON; STEEL).

cast iron Iron that contains roughly 2 to 4.5 percent CARBON. The carbon lowers iron's melting point. The molten iron can then be cast (poured into molds of the desired shape).

compound A mixed material that includes two or more ELEMENTS.

conductor In chemistry a material that allows heat or electricity to flow readily through it.

Damascus sword: See WOOTZ STEEL.

electricity A kind of power involving a flow of ELECTRONS, closely related to MAGNETISM.

electron A kind of tiny particle that is part of an ATOM. The flow of electrons is responsible for chemical REACTIONS, MAGNETISM, and ELECTRICITY.

elements The basic materials that make up every living and nonliving thing in the universe (112 of them are known so far, but more are being discovered). In an element all the ATOMS are alike.

erosion The wearing away of the Earth's crust by wind, rain, ice, and other natural forces. This can break up rock, freeing iron and other particles.

ferrum, ferric, ferrous The Latin word for iron is *ferrum*, abbreviated in chemistry as *Fe*. The names of iron-containing COMPOUNDS often begin with *ferric* or *ferrous*.

galvanized iron Iron coated with the ELEMENT zinc to prevent RUST.

hematite: See ORE.

hemoglobin A material in the body's red blood cells. It contains iron that picks up OXYGEN from the lungs and delivers it to the rest of the body.

Iron Age In archaeology the period when a culture began to use iron for its main tools and weapons.

limonite: See ORE.

magnetism A power of attraction between materials. Iron is easily magnetized. *Magnetite*, an iron-containing ORE, is a natural magnet.

magnetite: See ORE; MAGNETISM.

melting point The temperature at which a substance melts. Iron melts at 1,536 degrees Celsius (about 2,800 Fahrenheit).

metal A group of ELEMENTS that includes iron. Most metals are good CONDUCTORS, and they often easily form COMPOUNDS with other elements. Usually solid at room temperature, they can often be hammered into desired shapes (see WROUGHT IRON) or melted and poured into desired shapes (see CAST IRON).

meteorite A rock from space. Some meteorites are as much as 90 percent iron.

ore A natural material that contains a desired substance. The main iron-containing ores include the reddish-brown *hematite*, the black *magnetite* (see MAGNETISM), and the brownish *limonite*.

oxygen One of the main ELEMENTS in the universe. Necessary for SMELTING iron, it readily combines with iron, as in HEMOGLOBIN and RUST.

quenching: See TEMPERING.

reaction In chemistry a joining together or breaking apart of ELEMENTS or COMPOUNDS. Iron is strongly reactive, so it very easily combines with other materials, as in RUST.

rust A series of COMPOUNDS formed by iron and oxygen in the presence of water and air. Iron will rust unless protected (see GALVANIZED IRON; STEEL).

smelting The process of melting and purifying an ORE to separate out one or more desired METALS.

stainless steel: See STEEL.

steel An ALLOY of iron that contains less than 2 percent CARBON plus varying amounts of other ELEMENTS for different purposes. Rust-resistant steel is called *stainless steel*.

tempering Strengthening CAST IRON by slowly reheating it and then plunging it into cold liquid (*quenching*).

wootz steel A kind of strong early steel made in India and the Middle East. *Damascus swords* were made from it.

wrought iron Worked iron; that is, iron that is reheated and hammered into desired shapes.

On the Internet

The Internet has many interesting sites about iron. The site addresses often change, so the best way to find current addresses is to go to a search site, such as www.yahoo.com. Type in a word or phrase, such as "iron."

As this book was being written, websites about iron included:

http://www.steel.org/
American Iron and Steel Institute (AISI), offering information, articles, a learning center, links to related sites, and a glossary.

http://www.iss.org/
The Iron and Steel Society, offering publications about the history and modern technology of iron and steel.

http://www.ironews.com/
Iron News—The World of Wrought Iron, an online newsletter.

http://www.bethsteel.com/
Bethlehem Steel website, which offers information on modern steelmaking, plus many downloadable images, historical and current.

In Print

Your local library system will have various books on iron. The following is just a sampling of them.

The Coming of the Age of Iron. Theodore A. Wertime and James D. Muhly, eds. New Haven, CT: Yale University Press, 1980.

Franck, Irene M., and David M. Brownstone. *Manufacturers and Miners.* New York: Facts On File, 1989. Part of the Work Throughout History series.

Iron and Steel in the Nineteenth Century. Paul F. Paskoff, ed. 1989.; *Iron and Steel in the Twentieth Century.* Bruce E. Seely, ed. 1994. New York: Facts On File.

Lauffer, Randall Byron. *Iron and Your Heart.* New York: St. Martin's, 1993.

Mielczarek, Eugenie V., and Sharon Bertsch McGrayne. *Iron, Nature's Universal Element.* New Brunswick, NJ: Rutgers University Press, 2000.

Popplewell, Frank. *Iron and Steel Production in America.* New York: Routledge/Thoemmes Press, 1999.

Pounds, Norman J. G. *The Geography of Iron and Steel.* London: Hutchinson University Library, 1959.

Ricketts, John A. *History of Ironmaking.* Warrendale, PA: Iron and Steel Society, 2000.

Van Nostrand's Scientific Encyclopedia, 8th ed., 2 vols. Douglas M. Considine and Glenn D. Considine, eds. New York: Van Nostrand Reinhold, 1995.

Wertime, Theodore A. *The Coming of the Age of Steel.* Chicago: University of Chicago Press, 1962.

Iron

Index

Alabama 17
alloy 7, 18, 26, 30
alloy steel 26
aluminum 6
anemia 14
atoms 10, 30

bacteria 4, 15
basic oxygen furnace (BOF) 27–28
bellows 19, 22–23
Bessemer, Henry 26
Bethlehem Steel 23, 28
blacksmiths 6, 20, 24, 29–30
blast furnace 23–29
blood 13–15, 30
bloom 19–20, 22–23
bowl furnace 19
bridges 10, 25–26
bronze 18–20

carbon 5, 19, 21–22, 26, 30
cast iron 7, 21–22, 24–26, 30
charcoal 19, 21, 23–24
China 17, 22, 25
chlorosis 15
chromium 26
coke 23, 25, 27
colors 5, 7–8, 13–18, 20–21, 30
compass 11–12
compounds 7–10, 18, 30
conductors 6, 10, 30
construction 4, 10, 22, 25–26, 29
continuous casting 29
cooking 7, 26
copper 18–19
core of Earth 4, 6, 16
crust of Earth 4, 6, 17, 30
Cyprus 20
Czech Republic 20

Damascus swords 22, 30

Darby, Abraham 25

Egypt 17, 22
electric arc furnaces 28–29
electricity 6, 10, 12, 26, 28, 30
electromagnetism 12
electrons 10–11, 30
elements 6, 8, 10, 16, 27, 30
England 17, 25
enriched foods 14
erosion 17, 30

factories 25, 29
ferric (oxides) 8–9, 30
ferrous 8–9, 30
ferrum (Fe) 8–9, 30
fining 24
forging 29
France 17
furnaces 9, 19–22, 25–29

galvanized iron 9, 30
Germany 17, 19

hammering iron 6–7, 20, 22, 24, 30
heat 6–7, 9, 16–30
hematite 16–17, 30
hemoglobin 13, 30
Hephaestus 6

India 17, 22, 30
Industrial Revolution 25
ingots 29
Iron Age 5, 18–21, 30
Ironbridge 25
iron deficiency 14
iron horses 5, 26
iron overload 15

jewelry 19

Latin 9
limestone 23, 27
limonite 17, 30

lodestone 11–12
Luxembourg 17

magnetic resonance imaging (MRI) 12
magnetism 4–5, 7, 10–12, 30
magnetite 11, 16–17, 30
manganese 26
melting 9, 16–19, 21–24, 27, 30
melting point 19, 21–22, 30
metals 6–7, 9, 12, 30
meteorites 16, 19, 30
Middle Ages 9
Middle East 18–19, 30
mild steel 26
mining 7, 16–17
Minnesota 17
molds 7, 24–25, 29–30
molybdenum 26

navigation 12
Newfoundland 17
Newport Bridge 10
nickel 26
niobium 26
north 11–12

open-hearth furnaces 27–28
ores 16–17, 19, 23, 27, 30
oxygen 6, 8–9, 13, 19, 27–28, 30

painting 5, 9, 18
Paterson Iron Company 25
pig iron 23–24, 26–28
pipes 19
plants 4, 15
poles, magnetic 11–12
processing 7, 16
purity 7, 16

quenching 22, 30

railroads 5, 26

reactions 8–10, 30
recording tape 4, 8–9, 12
rolling mill 29
Romans 9, 20
rust 8–9, 26, 28, 30

scrap steel 12, 28–29
shaft (furnace) 19, 23
silicon 6, 26
slag 19, 21–22
smelting 5, 18–30
south 11–12
Spain 17–18
spinning machines 25
stainless steel 5, 26, 30
steel 4–5, 7, 9–10, 12, 22, 26–30
Sweden 17

tableware 5
tapping 23
television 12
tempering 22, 30
tin 5, 18, 26, 28
tin cans 5, 26, 28
tools 16, 18–22, 25, 30
tool steel 26
tungsten 26
Turkey 19
tuyeres 19

Ukraine 17

vanadium 26
vegetables 14
Venezuela 16
Vulcan 6

water 9, 12, 17, 22–23, 26, 29-30
weapons 5, 16, 18–22, 24, 30
Whitney, Eli 25
wood 12, 18, 19, 22, 25
wootz steel 22, 30
Wright of Derby, Joseph 6
wrought iron 20, 22, 26, 30

32

RECEIVED DEC 2 8 2004

$269.00 per st.